SHOOT THE MESSENGER

A POETRY & PHOTOGRAPHY COLLECTION

SHOOT THE MESSENGER

A POETRY & PHOTOGRAPHY COLLECTION

BY COREY BLACK

Published by BlackSince1982
12081 Natural Bridge Rd. Bridgeton, MO 63044

Cover and interior design by Corey Black
Cover Photography by Adrian Walker
Other Photography Credits: Alex White for DIM Productions, Teddy Blackmon for Bfree Paparazzi, Tyrone Day for Day Boy Customs and Pacia Elaine.
ISBN: 978-1312340404

Printed in the United States of America

For Gina

1

2

COREY BLACK

5

6

CONTENTS

9

RANDOM BLANK PAGE

JOT DOWN A GREAT IDEA

FOREWORD

YO!!!!
DO NOT SKIP THIS!!!
YOU MUST READ THIS!!!

If you're like me, you probably don't even bother reading the foreword and jump right into the meat of the book, but let's chill on that for now. Let's take a moment to reflect on why we are holding a poetry book in our hands right now. I say we, because I am with you, right now, at this very second. You and me are about to share my experiences… together.

I'm going to tell you things about me, you're going to open up to things about yourself, and we both are gonna try to figure out this thing called life. Sure, we may never come up with any good enough answers, except for the ones we already know, but that's fine. We are gonna get very acquainted with our thoughts and feelings and emotions, and all the other stuff hidden between these stanzas and bars. We are about to laugh together, cry together, and fall in love together. We are going to have conversations with

God. We're gonna fantasize and explore the facets of love. We are about to capture the little moments that we so often let get flushed away.

Oh, and how I could I forget that this book has pictures! PICTURES!! If you ask me, a book without pictures is like a sandwich without bread. Visual art is so dear to me and I wanted it to be a part of this book just to add a little more spice to the poetry. They say a picture is worth a thousand words, and I've always believed that I can show you better than I can tell you. There are still certain images burnt into my memory that haven't faded, as vivid as the moment they occurred, and I wanted you to see some of the things that I see, even if you weren't there with me. That's the reason I write, so we can see things as I see them… as art.

Anyway… this is my first collection of poetry. I only incorporated the works I liked, just to spare you from any boring and garbage poems. Also, as we are reading, you may hear my voice in the words, that's absolutely normal. Don't get freaked out at all, I told you, we are doing this together. Teamwork! (Can I say lol or nah? Not really sure how forewords go).

Sidebar: Rules kinda suck.

I say that to say this: This book doesn't have any real structure. It's pretty raw and I just kinda made it feel as authentic as possible so you know it's real. We won't worry ourselves over sentence fragments and words that don't even exist, just go with the flow. That will make it easier on us.

Enjoy the journey. Enjoy this experience, and let's just have an awesome time doing it.

15

IT STARTS
WITH
A DREAM

17

THE INTRO

Shorty walked with two bags.
One had his future, while the other had his trash.

The only problem was he made an error on the tags, and he threw away his fate

So now he walks around frustrated, carrying dead weight.

He never planned on getting older.

His main chick, told him quick, "If you don't quit the whole relationship is over."

Now you never see him sober, it's hard to keep his eyes up
Ran inside her womb and left a seed deep inside her

Now baby boy is about to have a baby girl, but he can barely take care of himself

Still, you never see him beggin' for help

Plus everybody thinks he's cool, the flyest dude in the school
He gives his sister a couple of dollars like he's paying for her college

Which he is, because as long as she's getting money from him
Then she isn't sexing everybody and trying to get it from them

And that's worth more than scholarships, he's proud of his influence
Never truant from her questions like a teacher and a student

"Why do good girls like bad boys?" Blame it on their brothers.
Get in good with the daddies and be sweeter to the mothers

Those candy coated roses weren't cheaper by the dozens
He tried his best to do his best, but couldn't keep up with his cousin

Not a worry in the world, but that was about to change soon
Played the songs of their soul all on the same tune

On that Sunday afternoon, in the early month of June
When his pops heart stopped and he woke up in the Upper Room

So consumed by the fact, and the irony of the act
That is was Father's Day at that, and he's do anything to bring him back

And you can see it in his eyes as his world gets colder
R.I.P. tattoo over the chip on his shoulder

Had to lay down his burdens, he was cursing at the alter
The pastor was a daddy with a house full of daughters

He tried his best to stay away from the bullshit
Got a calling, but he had to stay away from the pulpit

Just suppose he was supposed to close his seven holes
The two for his ears and the two for his nose

Don't forget his eyes, so he's left with his mouth
Holding in his last breath and vows to never let it out

But by would he want to die, when he could ride in the sky?
He learned how to fly, he was just too afraid to try

He just turned 25, and he's living for the moment
His destiny is foggy, so he treats it like and omen

'Til they threw him on a cross, his demons fed him to the Romans
Now he's roamin', and atonement is a week away, but his home is

The valley of the shadow, right under the ram's hoof
He was born in a tent by the river like Sam Cooke

BRKNHRTD

That cold stare that she gave me when she looked me in my eyes

The trust was built atop a foundation full of lies

Disguised the blue skies with gray clouds on her Sunday

I knew eventually this day was bound to happen one day

And some play games disregarding every rule

But when the clock runs out it's so hard to play it cool

Love without limits, I never seen it coming

Never crying over spilled milk but now the tears are running

Dumbfounded by your actions

THERE GOES MY BABY

Little Miss Sunshine, she takes away his rain
On her flight to DC, nothing takes away the pain of her absence,

Finding it so hard to believe
That she's gone, and he didn't get a chance to see her leave

No kisses goodbye and he tried to make it work
This is the kind of loneliness that can shake the Earth and it hurts,

But not as much as what he goes through with her mother
On the speakerphone telling her how much her daddy loves her

Her tender kisses are the only thing he misses
He's a slave for her, her commands are his wishes

DON

Looking at the man, with the microphone in his hand.

The one with the afro that makes the house dance.

Thick, shaded glasses that cover his eyes,

That tacky suit and tie that he makes look so jive.

A cool mellow voice, so calm and so smooth,

Teaching the whole world, to move how we move.

Life is a lovely melody, and our actions are the rhyme,

But if you want to dance to the music,

You've gotta stand in the Soul Train Line.

COREY BLACK

THIS JUST LOOKED LIKE
A GREAT PLACE TO
PUT MY LOGO… CARRY ON

LEANIN'

Slow motion, relaxing in the ride

The breeze on my face got me feeling so alive

Never felt better than this, no worries

Time flies by, I'm never in a hurry

No rush, take my time 'til I get it right

On a joyride, on the highway of life

Full tank of gas with the Lord on my side

It's such a better ride when u letting God drive

Road less traveled, but I'm gonna make it home

Searching for myself, but I'll never be alone

Looking for the power and I made it to the source

No collisions on the course and I'm riding with The Force

And nothing's gonna stop me, doing what it takes

See the limits on the speed, so I'm pumping on the brakes

Amazed by the grace, you can see it in my eyes

Watching all the days of my life passing by as
I'm leanin' to the side

WHEN YOU CHANGE YOURSELF

—

THE WORLD CHANGES WITH YOU

29

REVOLUTION

The Revolution will not be seen on 52 inch screens in hi-definition

My definition of change is not the same as President Obama's

While I was training for Iraq, you were home watching dramas on TNT

See, we know dramas too

The Marines found Saddam, and the hunt for Osama is through

There were no weapons of mass destruction

There is nothing new under the sun

We'll find the Promised Land through logistics

Redefining the classic blueprints in accordance to keep anything vintage futuristic

Never losing our way, focusing on the destinies foreseen by our forefathers

That promised our people three lonely words: We Shall Overcome

I'm so sick of seeing this same episode, rewinding this rerun

What's Happening Now, is that too many of these brothers wanna be like Rerun

All that dancing stuff is cool, but it don't get you through school

'So you're sitting at home, and you're watching you life pass you by'

Ask me why they made the switch from analog to digital

It's the same distance between being religious and being spiritual

And I refuse to stay peaceful in the middle of the riot
Even David grabbed a rock when he battled Goliath

So I'm thinking slingshot, these words and our voices are our bullets

And I ain't got a problem with lettin'
that thang pop, lettin' that thang rock

Because they are capitalizing cultures by corrupting commerce

Through commercialized sponsors just to keep commercials commercial

If they can con some of the consumers, we'll never notice the switch

They'll keep the real artist broke, and make the wack rappers rich

And they say, "You ain't gon' make a stack trying to save the people black, you better do something about money, cash, cars, or clothes..."

No, what I'll do is invite them to my shows, so they can see for themselves that the revolution will not be televised

Nor will it be uploaded to facebook, YouTube, twitter, instagram, or blogs

The Revolution will begin inside

When you start looking for God.

SHE LIVES IN WATER

I met you in my last forever
I met you in a past forever
It's obvious we'll last forever
And forever may just be a reoccurring now
Maybe that's why it feels like we've been here before
Why your presence is so familiar
Why your kiss feels like home
Why your touch is so known

Why I've never seen a red flag, alert, or danger

The stars align you came from a different space and time
You exercise my mind and allow me to explore life
I implode around you
The entire fucking universe surrounds you

You love me like God does

You're everything that God was
Before western religion
Loving you eternally was my greatest decision
Baptized in her ambition
She lives in water
As true as sky blue and a reflection of the heavens

Sweet yellows and Oshuns oh you are so beautiful

BUILD & DESTROY

Don't tear me down yet

Let that eternal linger

There's no need to feed the belly of the full with bullshit

Taking for granted the taste of the fast

If yo' mind is already swine, then I know you'll go fork that pork

And drinking Pepsi out of Coca-Cola bottles don't mean you can pass the challenge either

I challenge you to try to fix it before it's broke

Not while the conditions are working well, hell

If the shoe fits, then get yo' ass on the good foot

And walk a mile in mine

Otherwise, otherwise, otherwise

You're just passin' time

'til that new shit becomes figments and fragments

Losing my direction to memory lane because a lot of these lames

Are fucking up a good game

Like a blind umpire in the World Series

Can't finish 'til we win a pennant though...

But it's getting on my nerves dog, they keep throwing me these curve balls

And I may have 99 problems, but a pitch ain't one

So I'll just adjust to that real, and let it do what it's supposed to do

And that's live, build and destroy.

THE DAY SHE LEFT

The fruition of my dreams

Out of all the women I've seen, she's remains the hottest

Surrounded by a thousand Sheba's and Cleopatra's

But what's a queen to a goddess? Nothing

So no thing could, should, or would ever make me leave.

Leave it up to time and space to make us break

The weight of too much time and not enough space

Or too much space and not enough time

Too many cloudy days and not enough shine

Too many moons have passed

And not enough room to smash in a few precious second

That she longed for everyday

Regretting every moment I stayed away

Maybe stopping the hands of time would've made her stay

Still remember every word she left on the letter

The day she left.

VAGUE FLASHES

A blaze of crimson light

Telling its own story

Becoming a sight to dwell upon

Remembered by forgetful eyes

That patiently waited for a New One

We knew some day the dreams would come true

So we begged for longer days and shorter nights

Vague flashes that trickle over the galaxies for eons

Rapid Eye Movements, lace the memories with neon

The melodies razzle as the rays dazzle and dance

On the fallen feathers of angel wings

Learning lessons from these florescent blessings

That drifts across vacant corners of my imagination

And I see the shadows of my pain

Blinded by the lightning bolts dancing in the rain

I wonder how these thunderstorms made it to my brain

I thought I had my umbrella but I must've left it on the plane

And I would complain, but I trained myself to refrain

The precipitation hopefully can wash away the stain

Or maybe put the flame out from the fire by the tree

When the lightning hit the Earth, a couple miles away from me

Shocking isn't it?

How little sparks of light can turn around your life.

A FOOL WILL
BELIEVE
HIS OWN LIES

PRETENDER

Daydreaming and I'm thinking bout my past
Looking back at all the reasons why They didn't last
Maybe I was selfish, a victim of my vanity
Dealing with depression and borderline insanity
Or maybe I was blinded by the lies and deceit
had me under the impression that it was ok to cheat
Long as I didn't get caught
Cause that's what I was taught
I thought that I was cool but I was
Lying to my heart

INVISIBLE NO MORE

Sister I will be your brother
The guardian sent by mother
Protection unconditionally
I will provide for you
Baby girl I will ride for you
Make sure you keep your head to the sky for you
I will see to it that you will be invisible no more.

MIAMI

Round trips and reservations
Request a few days off for vacation
We really gotta get away soon
Maybe front desk could send crepes and mimosas to our room
For the weekend keep the city out of our reach
And we can drink Tequila, sunrise on the beach
Toes in the sand, you holding my hand
Everything about this trip goes according to plan

ROMANTIC SECURITY

Bands will make her dance
Bands will make her dance
But that 401k will make her stay
If you pay a couple bills
That will make her chill
So hypothetically speaking it's all trickin' still
Don't matter if you got it or you don't
A few woman will stick around if you ain't got a job, but most of them won't
Sure, they'll stay to help you get back on your feet in hopes that you do better
But if you don't attempt to make an effort to change the situation she'll be sayin "I should've knew better"
and after that 83rd ultimatum she gon' bounce like Bankhead, or shake like Harlem
There ain't no romance without finance so if your finances are a problem
the best way to solve them is to solve them.
Go get a job.

SOON COME

I been broken, I been torn
Like they cursed the day that I was born
But I know that this trouble won't last long
Mama told me it gets better after dawn
Lord knows I'll see my heaven before I'm gone
Soon come, just gotta make it through my storm

RIDE BY

New days
New mercies and new praise
Let the windows of the whip down
A sweet sultry sound
Pouring in an abundance of blessings glad it's over and done
And the summer is so young
Long winters get so cold
But that struggle was getting so old
Story often told, but
We riding now
All the storms are hiding now
They come and go properly
So don't rely on probably
Just be ready
The most high has a plan prepared, so why cry?
Almost gave up but stay prayed up
and never saw my blessing fly by

DRIFT

Sailing away
Drifting off a memory of you and I
Caught up in a superficial moment in time
waiting for the son and the moon to collide
Praying that you find me in my dreams tonight
Woke up to the essence of your beautiful smile

VIRGO STATE OF MIND

I'm a Virgo, which means I'm allergic to fuck-shit.

I'm a Virgo, which means I have no time for mediocrity.

I'm a Virgo, which means I'm not perfect, but everything about me is.

I'm a Virgo, which means I'm always right, even when I'm wrong.

I'm a Virgo, which means my confidence is sometimes overshadowed by my excellence.

I'm a Virgo, which means I'm compatible with people that don't understand me.

I'm a Virgo, which means I am always thinking about thoughts that need to be thought about.

I'm a Virgo, which means I'm technically as dope as Michael Jackson, Beyonce, and Nas.

I'm a Virgo, you're welcome.

NATURAL WOMAN

It's something about the way that you look when you look at me;
if looks could kill I would tell the jury to charge you with Murder in the first degree

See, I'm well aware of the fact that this whole look that you've got going on was premeditated

What Elevated your intentions, was your one last quality control check before you departed your apartment and confessed to the mirror, "I'm killing it tonight, knowing damn well I was gonna be in your line of sight.

Am I right? If I'm wrong, then I won't carry on, but it still doesn't negate the fact that you got it going on.

... You are looking so fly, and I don't even know why.

Not exactly quite sure if it's the Christian Dior, Michael Kors, or Tom Ford, or maybe it's that sexy, nonchalant attitude that you giving off that's translating you're slightly engaged, but kinda bored.

If u wanna be entertained, I'll make some time for it

Oh, you fancy huh?
Nails done, hair done, everything did.
And you're just tryin' to do everything big.

Like Afros with the pick with black fist, standing in the midst of all these chocolate sisters looking like an abyss, at best you still abreast with the goddesses

And even though you're modest, every single things about your right now is
Considered the hottest I'm just being honest

You make a brother want to ask questions because I'm really trying to figure out what's going on in, out and around your head

Sweet mother Aretha this queen's fine this natural woman has losing track of time
In the meantime have you ever seen time stand still

because I swear the hands on the clock didn't move
when u walked in the room

Question:
Do have to wake up extremely early to get your hair that curly?
And do you ever feel like people be hatin' whenever u get it straightened?
Or do you not even trip over your hair at all?

You've got me in awe and I just wanna watch you glow.
Whether its fried, died laid to side
Shaved, bangs, a bun, braids or bob
twist out dreds shaved heads and locks
Or even just a simple wash and go

All you're worried about is keeping up with the maintenance and maintaining its condition
conditioning it for twenty minutes with your shower cap on
but by the time that it's done its looking like the lights got cut off and Ameren just cut the power back on

Your beauty is an extent of love coming into fruition
you're beautiful, and its kinda dope that God is your beautician

QUEEN

The spell you put men under
It's hypnotic and makes one wonder
If you were transported by a fleet of seraphim angels or did the ancestors find it necessary to cloak you with the beauty of eternal sunshine
Some find it hard to believe in ancient myths and Mt. Olympus, but with you those doubts become droughts whenever I see you out
recognize a goddess when you see one
And if you're not familiar with the traits of an empress, easy, she's one
I'm talking about you, not silly playa lines or game,
More like, please play Alicia Keys, 'she don't know my name'
Looking for you with no map, but still I could find you
Cut from the cloth of queens
Amazed by the design of whoever designed you

55

MY MARINE CORPS DAYS, OORAH!

ON STAGE, DOIN' MY THING

HUMBLE
THYSELF

KILL OR
BE KILLED

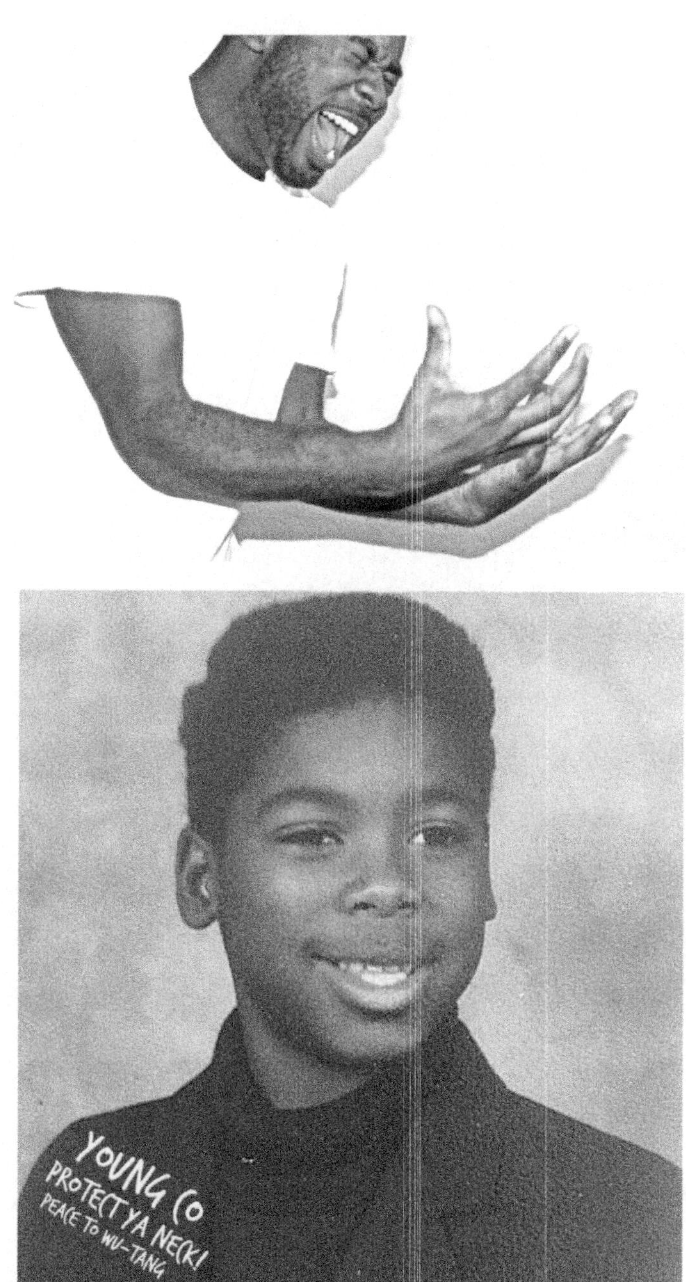
YOUNG CO
PROTECT YA NECK!
PEACE TO WU-TANG

FOREVER
HAITI

Harlem
Board here
Out

HEAVEN IS IN HER EYES

I looked in your eye

Took in your high

Hook, line, sinking
if you could stop blinking

Then I could stop thinking of ways to gaze at artificial rays that don't produce half the light at the sight that comes from your soul's windshields or windows

Your hypnotic optics are sunrises over the tropics

And I feel like Osiris when I look in your iris and you become my Isis

And we could be as big as the letter E is on the eye test

Because her eyes disguise the skies and I decide to be her disciple
better yet, pupil when we connect pupils

Dilate my stigmatism
your cataracts speak blissful vocabularies

And the words heard could convert a Muslim into a Hebrew
Eye candy so sweet it gives a blind man a sweet tooth

Far from transparent or see thru
I'd never break u or break up

Very little eye shadows and not a lot of make up

Those lovely eyes, but my eyes love too
and since god is love, then I see the god in you

And as choirs and masses sing hymns from your lashes
I'm captured in raptures that fracture the flashes before my eyes as the story of my life passes

No stresses or strains but her eyes are like dope and I feel like an addict
But this ain't no magic, no hocus pocus

Staring into her eyes until mine lose focus cause she's my fantasy, every piece of my dream
No irritation, but for me her eyes are like Visine and it makes me want to sing

"Heavens eye view is not above you it's at your eye level that's why I love you"

And baby girl is just like me
but her eyes keep me in check like pair of Nikes

And it's highly unlikely that I'll be the cause of her crying
Cause God would never allow for there to be a flood in Zion.

Heaven is in her eyes.

WHERE I CAME FROM

Reflections of everything neglecting does to the spirit
Poured inside every lyrics are the voices of wrong
choices that manifested into healed scabs so we still
laugh at the meaningless errors smiling in the mirrors,
puddles and dark glasses, my heart clashes at the
thought of all the roads I've crossed before I called
myself a man
Before I told myself I can
In a world that's soul objective is to knock me down
But nothing can stop me now except myself
Numb fingers stretched out to empty pockets to help
myself in this cold world
Reminiscent of the euphoric utopia that only existed as
a child
Trying to be tamed while still out in the wild
I smile, but only to cover the pain I'm ashamed off
Lost in this world, but never forgetting where I came
from

12:34AM

I just wish that I could hold you
I just wish I would've told you
I never meant to leave you
I really thought I didn't need you
But now I'm feeling empty
And the devil's trying to tempt me
The pain level is so high
It feels like I'm about to die
Is this how broken hearts beat?
Is this the reason why I can't sleep?

LIBRA

They say you can't leave a Libra
Especially when she's balancing those scales so well
Teeter-tottering in between heaven and hell
She is so real
She believes in everything she sees In him
Wit her pecan skin blue jeans and tims
If they ain't fuckin' wit, then her she ain't fuckin' wit them
The definition of ambition she was born to ball
So it's no coincidence that she was born in fall
Majestic like the opal in her birthstone
Making the whole earth moan
Punch drunk love, I'm glad she's not sober
Celebrating everyday with young Miss October

I DONT KNOW

Can't feel the love
Can taste the hate
No one to trust
Brand new mistakes

So confused
Distorted thoughts
Misunderstood
Soul is lost

Can't find a way
Can't get it right
Blind in the day
Can't see at night

Overload
Won't take a break
Can't slow me down
Procrastinate
You don't know about us
We dot don't about them
I don't know about you
I don't know about him
I don't know about me

76

I don't know about her
I don't know about shit
But I don't even care

3:00AM

Why am I up this late thinking about you?
Can't fall asleep and I don't know what I'm about to do.
Looked at some old pictures,
didn't realize I missed u so much.
We looked so damn good together girl,

What in the hell happened to us?

I could say it's my fault, you can blame it on you, don't matter who it was.
When it's all said and done, it's 3:00 in the morning and I'm missing your touch.
Pay a visit in your sleep right now,
Hope you're dreaming about me right now,
everything we used to be right now
Wish that you were holding me right now.

THINK OF ME

Not sure what it is she does to me but I love it
This woman has my heart and every beat of it
Don't be another addiction
I don't need a new habit
This don't make a lot of sense
A million broken promises
Can't listen to what Simon Says
And I'm riding 'round and I'm writin' this
Don't even know what time it is
But I wish that I could call and say
Baby how was your day?
Did somebody make you smile?
Did anybody make you laugh
and did you think about me?
I wanted to call and say
that I think about you everyday
Wish I would've never walked away
and it's destroying me.

REFLECTIONS OF COURTNEY

Assigned by God to protect this angel.

A guardian, chosen.

Her saying "he is the one."

Honor.

Duty, to explain to her what love is and how it should move.

Required, to kill the imaginary monsters under her bed.

Tea parties and fashion shows.

She teaches me to be a king.

Lifted.

Magically kissing the pain of her stumbles away.

She identifies my strength to that of the giants.

Love, at first sight, euphoric.

She redefined my purpose.

Giver of my most sacred title:

Father.

BLACK MUSIC

It began with the rhythm

The warm vibrations bursting through the blanket of darkness

God was singing out into the void let there be this and let there be that

Atoms were colliding before Adam came out the dirt

The motion of the oceans were swaying to the shores as the trees threw their branches "in the air and waved em like they just didn't care"

And the birds flirted with chirps of the crickets and somewhere in the solitude of silence

We began listening to our heart.

The pulse of life that beat like a djembe in our soul

It began with the rhythm.

It began with the beat.

It began with the drum.

GOLDEN GATES

My daddy favorite song

He told me play it for him on the day we send him home

Tell Bird to pour another round

And make it kinda strong

Cause it's Friday and my father said the week was way too long

Conquian in the kitchen with my mama

He told me stay away from messy women that love drama

Pour a chevas regal

Yeah, Arnold's in the house

For five minutes and thirty seconds

He lets his soul come out

HAPPINESS
IS FREE
—
BUT YOU PAY
FOR SHIPPING
AND HANDLING

PRISONER

Trapped
In an asylum of bitterness
Yearning for a dose of sunlight
Haunted by the demons of an unforgiving memory
Shackled and defeated
Wrapped in velvety cuffs and plush restraints
Freedom's illusion
It comforts me

-HAIKUS-

The circle of life
What goes around comes around
Karma is a bitch

The vicious cycle
Three hundred sixty-five days
Yearlong love affairs

Love without limits
Dance like no one is watching
Fear does not exist

When everything fails
And you can't find the answers
Listen to your heart

THE YEAR

The cold winter's brisk wind

Ignited the bliss when

We began kissing

Long before we finished singing Auld Lang Synge

All games aside, I knew this love would never worry

Feeling too weak,

Like fourteen days into February

But too hard for Hallmark cards and roses

Yet the madness catches up to us as we March forth

No looking back

This ain't magic okay

And your friend's eyes are getting greener

Than St. Patrick's Day parades

And to say that April showers fools

For falling in love at first sight

Like waiting for May flowers

To set sail on my ocean to spring on and explore

Are we moving too fast too soon?

My first day of summer, my last day of June

The dog days

Wait

Love hurts when you try

But we could be in the sky

Like fireworks in July

And now you want to act a fool

Because I'm taking you back to school

Sticking to the fundamentals of this relationship

But the labor that you have put me through has got me ready to fall back

You've painted on my face

I've been tricking for your treats

Sweeter than potato pies and pineapple baked ham

Thanks for giving me a run for my money

I'm such a dummy

Stuffing all that poison inside my tummy

Packing on pounds that I didn't even need

Had the nerve to try and leave three days before Christmas Eve

Oh, Holy Night

The stars are brightly shinin' and I'll quit all my whinin'

And make a resolution to not fall in love again

It's played out

Stayed out the dating scene all year

Figured this party was just the break I needed

Until she walked back in

And got under my skin

And this ends the cold winter's brisk wind
That ignited the bliss
When we began kissing
Long before we finished singing Auld Lang Synge

WHEN YOU SEE ME

When you hear me or when you see me
It's a testimony that somebody needs me

Some people get a calling only once in their life
But it's like I hear the voice of God when I get called to a mic

And it tells me to get on my feet and walk to the light
And show the rest of the world why my talk is so bright

Why I shine when I rhyme and I barely am tryin'
How the prize in my eyes are inferno and diamond

Fire and ice
It gets me higher than kites
I'll battle squires and knights
I'll be a rider for life

For now

I take these calculated steps

Preparing to scorch

A man on fire

I am burning

When you touch me…. Don't touch me

I'm burning

I'm hot, sizzling, blazing, pay attention

If you can't stand the heat, stay out of the kitchen

You'll see me out here walking

I be on my mission

I do this for the love, but get paid off commission

I do it God's way, the heavens gave me permission

I can squeeze an entire church service into a couple of minutes

All I have is a couple of minutes

I try not to lose my voice

Some people are given options

But I don't have a choice

I do this for my culture
I am a slave for my people
And only slaves can free slaves
So it may seem like I am an equal
But I am more than meets the eye
I transform into an eagle

This life is just a movie
And you don't get a sequel

So while you're looking, watch me
And I pray that you see a blessing, when you see me

FOR AMIRI

How did you leave?

Did you drift away on a saxophone riff?

Did you float off on a blues note from Miles?

Did you hear Malcolm whisper your name?

Did you wander off into one of your poems?

Is that where I can find you?

Are you somewhere familiar?

Will I find you in Harlem, resurrecting the renaissance?

Are you somewhere, are you somewhere?

Somewhere in between the Book of Romans and one of your essays?

Where can I find you?

Are you lingering around the 7th verse of the 2nd chapter of Genesis?

Are you somewhere?

Somewhere in between the Book of Hebrews and a Donald Goines novel?

Where can I find you?

Are you in the midst of the storm telling the devil to get behind you?

Are you somewhere?

Is you somewhere?

Is you in between the pit and the palace?

Can I find you loitering around Marcus Garvey's breakfast or Martin Luther's lunch?

Ain't you somewhere in the motherland?

Are you somewhere with the gods?

Is you somewhere in Pharaoh's tomb or on David's alter?

Will I find you? Will you find me?

Telling my people to get behind me

Fully aware of our struggle so there's no need to remind me.

Is you gon be here at the end when we all together?

Brother Amiri, live forever.

SCHOLAR

I am the dream of Martin Luther King

My words do not speak as loud as my actions

I am pro-active

Radioactive

I move in waves

With a reassuring pride my ancestors are able to rest peacefully in their graves

Proud of me

Fulfillment of prophecy

Foresight of what was to come

I am the answer

Of me they could be no prouder

I am the academic, the apprentice, the student, the scholar

I am a 3.0, 3.2, and 3.5

I am 4.0, I am a full ride

I am the songs from the cage that little bird gave

I am the prize in the eyes

I am Maya Angelou's Still I Rise

Word for word, verbatim

I am Frederick Douglass' handshakes with Abraham Lincoln

I am Nat Turner's revolt against demons

I am Marcus Garvey's prestige on the harbors of New York City

I am Fred Hampton's charisma through revolution

I am Brother Malcolm's conversations with Elijah Muhammad

I am knowledge of life and self

I am the voice in a silent auditorium

I am the speech of every valedictorian

I walk with legends and giants

I build foundations on broken nations

In all of my battles I triumph, win or lose

I am victory

I am the hard work it takes to be great

I am every night you've stayed up late

100

I am the reason easy work is worthless

No days off

Motivated

I put the unity in community

Come together

I am the vision of a brighter day

Focused

The keys I hold open all doors

Power of education

I am the future

I am future

I am only bound by imagination

Limitless

I am fearless

I am phenomenal

I am love

I am black

I am beautiful

I am blessed

I am you

SHINE

Blind to the sights but I see the sounds around me

A free spirit that was lost, but I'm glad the angels found me

Clinching to their wings, the things I've seen could make cataracts lean

These sore eyes, poor guys didn't know what hit 'em

Silent voice in my head screaming, "GO GET 'EM"

Let's move, safe havens and rescue missions

It's impossible to deny the work of God in the middle of a transitional storm

The traditional norm is jaded and faded by fools creating their own dance

Dancing to the beat of different djembe and congo masters

Hands become slaves, and slave become kings

After all of the field work is done, we built Earth, so rebuild Earth then run

To the heavens, children of the tribes that lost their land but kept their faith

Take it to the alter with weary hearts and tired tongues

Singing praising 'til my lungs breakdown, taking him for every breath I breathe

I leave it in God's palms, and fall back until spring comes back

It's a new day, but you still can't rush the sunrise, so lift every voice and say:

"Let There Be Light"

Weeping only endures for the night, so smile a little longer

And what doesn't kill you makes you stronger

And what doesn't break you makes you who you are

So take it easy, one day at a time

This little light of mine, I'm gonna let it shine

NEVER
NOT BE
WEIRD

CONNECTED

We could be connected like the rope in double-dutch

Like such

As much as the crush I had on Ann Gibson in the first grade

In the nurses office, broken hearted, first-aid

Played

Sometimes I feel like she didn't even know me

I was in the same class as her little sister Toni

Tony

Tone

It never rains in Southern Calif-----

LIES! It does rain in San Diego

Now try to put that together like a shoebox full of Lego pieces

Praying you never run out of the flat ones

Talent show, for her I performed like a little Michael Jackson

Kicks, spins, moonwalks, tip-toe stance

All eyes were on me like everyone was learning how to dance

I tried to cater to her ego, but it varied

Addicted to this Aries, halos angel wings and fairies

It's scary, but the fear never lasts as long as it seems

The only time that we touch is when she visits in my dreams

I wake up, feeling better than I did before tomorrow

And it's such a beautiful day; I hope the sun lets me borrow

A little of his shine, because the whole world is mine

But I would trade it in for just a small fraction of her time

2/4, common denominate her ½

The little things I did, like when she was mad, I'd make her laugh

Now, and cry later

Say hello to all the haters

After while with crocodiles or go to Florida with the Gators like Tebow

Shotgun formations, seeking through her channels for a brand new radio station

My tender, hopefully she remembers, the taste of Sweet November

When she became a member, even though I'm nervous

"Good evening, I'll be at your service"

Enlisted

Because she said Marines did it better

And if it aint raining, then it aint training

So these sheets are getting wetter

Trying to pull myself together and never say never

Not until I've seen forever, have you ever seen forever?

Have you ever seen heaven?

You could be my reverend, pastor, bishop

Vinegar and hyssop, I thirst for your kisses

To worsen these conditions, I'm trying to use these scriptures just so I can paint these pictures.

Winter

Winner, winner.

No chicken dinner.

Tried to double down on that 8 of diamonds and 3 of spades praying that she would King me

Blackjack, checkerboards, playing all of her games

Just so she could put me inside of her heart's Hall of Fame

Shame, low down and dirty

Why should she hurt me?

She told me 20 is the new 30, so it'll never be too early for us to stop throwing rocks

Hopscotch on my heart, and she doesn't condone the knots

She ties inside of my stomach, all of these grown caterpillars

I never wanted to be the other guy, and she was my butterfly

And we could fall in love and die on Neveruary 32nd

Or March 4th for some, I know that sounds dumb

But it still comes from the drum beats by my lungs

She could've been my one, my numero uno

I could be her baby-daddy, she could be my Juno

Listen to these true note, legacy like blues notes

Popeye and Olive Oil, I'm still fighting off these Blutos

FREEDOM

We are trying to save the world one prayer at a time

IN a time when we only shine when the clouds are the thickest

As one percent of the riches are held at ransom

We fight to rewrite a new national anthem

Buried deep within these anacreontics are testimonies

Tears that mourn the fall of democracy

And we cannot see the break of the new day

For our hailed pride drowned in the abyss of the twilight

Certain that it is always darkest before dawn

We are awaken by the elaborate rings of freedom

Our liberties echo in the halls of justice

And we realize it is just us

Armed with picket signs and voices

Declaring that we be heard by a deaf machine

One that only understands the language of a ballot

Casting votes into a lake of desire

Our hopes rest in the hands of The American Experiment

For the land of the free and the home of the brave

Has become the real estate of the rich, and the home of the slave

United We Stand, Divided We Fall

We will lay down our lives

Just to Occupy a Wall

MY GREATEST LYRIC

She's becoming my greatest lyric, she is my flow

That soothing finesse that illuminates all of my words, she is my glow

My light, that breaches through the solitudes of my mind

And streams radiance to the deepest part of my imagination

She fills me, she really feels me

As complex as I am, she gets me

6.8 billion Brilliant brains on the planet, but she picks me

And she likes me, more than people like my facebook statuses

From the top of my head to the roughness of my feet calluses

She accepts me, for what I am and for what I can become

And no matter how infinite she makes me feel, she will always and forever be the one

She stands alone, but I manage to never leave her lonely

The opposite of phony, the epitome of only

The standard of quality and essence, her beauty resides

In regions so high that she makes the heavens squint their eyes

And she tries for nothing, so effortlessly

She can look at me and read the lost scriptures written on my soul

And she can translate the language of the angels with her kisses

Amazing is her being, her ever-fascinating aura

In a complexion set in the array of 10,000 sunsets, she gives me poetry

Dazzling sonnets and majestic hymns drawn out on Egyptian papyrus in hieroglyphics

Rhythmic orchestras sketched in compositions that channel through the paradox of my heart

She can whisper the secret of life with her smile

As the sounds of holiness echo in her laughter

She is my Queen

She is my love

She is my poetry

She is becoming my greatest lyric

REIGN FALL

Precision connections of the lights scattered across the dark sky

The stars aren't too far apart especially when you've learned how to protect the spots

Colored in books throughout the ages in pages built for the babies to connect the dots

Gotta crawl before you walk and we never stuttered before we talk

Choose our words wisely

So let it be written exactly how it's done

The spoils of the victor are spoiled because we've already won

Long the before the race ever started

Hate the lionhearted

But love our intentions

We are the cure for the affliction

And the answer for when the game calls

So be prepared for the glory

Drenching you in this reign fall

WRITE SOME POETRY

If you got inspired to write, use this space to pour your soul

WRITE SOME MORE POETRY

Keep it coming. Write about something beautiful you saw today.

KEEP WRITIN'!

Do you remember your dream last night? What was it about?

WRITE IT DOWN!!

Are you waiting for a breakthrough? Write your vision, every detail. Meditate on it, and let the universe handle the rest.

Made in the USA
Coppell, TX
15 February 2022